I0625469

Goals

Achieve Your Goals Now with PowerLists™

By Chris A. Baird

Goals: Achieve Your Goals Now with PowerLists™

Copyright © 2021 - All rights reserved. No part of this book may be reproduced in any form or by any means without permission in writing from the publisher, CAB Publishing. Please read the full disclaimer at the end of this book.

This book was self-published with the amazing help of Self-Publishing Made Easy Now! [1] . You can grab a free copy of the checklist that started my journey here: FREE Self-Publishing Checklist [2] .

[1] https://selfpublishingmadeeasynow.com/xpjv
[2] https://selfpublishingmadeeasynow.com/free_checklist

Table of Contents

1 - Introduction

This book is the first book in the bestselling PowerLists™ book series. Each PowerList™ book is designed to help you get more out of life.

Why This Book?

I wrote this book in order to help you better structure your life so that you can achieve your short- and long-term goals. Each topic could be written as a separate book. However, my goal is to provide enough information to get you up and running on the road to reaching your goals.

I am excited about helping you make your goals a reality. I've seen far too many people over the years frittering away their time and money because their goals were unclear. Each year they seemed no closer to achieving what they were capable of accomplishing.

How To Use This Book

It is impossible for anyone to implement all of the suggestions I have in this book. However, if my tips help you get any aspect of your goal evaluation, setting, and achievement in place, I will have succeeded in the purpose of this book. Try out the different tips and see what works and what doesn't for you. Making any progress towards our goals can be the catalyst to bigger and better changes in your life.

Which Goals Are in Focus?

The scope of this book will work for any goal. This is the beauty of the tools I am going to share with you. It doesn't matter what type of goal you wish to achieve. By applying these simple steps, you will come to believe you already possess everything you need. The only thing lacking is a method or system to get yourself moving. That is what I am here for. I hope you will find this book useful.

The book will explain the steps necessary to build your own PowerLists™. Typical examples of PowerLists™ are presented at the end of relevant chapters. You can also use the Excel list templates[3] . I start each chapter with a struggle I experienced in that key area and the questions I needed to

[3]http://www.powerlists.org/B01L02

answer to achieve my goals.

At a deep level, we really aren't different. We all experience struggles and must figure out what we are going to do about them, if anything. I hope this book will give you the best of what I have learned and am still learning regarding setting and reaching goals.

2 - Getting Started

After having twice switched majors in college, I had no vision for where I was headed. I had worked hard in high school to get into the Air Force Academy. Now that I was there, I didn't have a game plan for what should come next.

I suppose the idea was to graduate and then figure something out. However, there was something lacking: a clear goal, something which I was working toward. Up to this point I had made all my decisions based on what I thought would be useful later on, but I had no vision or direction. Where was I heading? What did I want to achieve?

No Quick Fix

You are probably reading this book because you want to get control of your life. Well, the first thing I want to get out of the way right up front is that *this isn't going to be easy.*

There is no button you can press to watch your life get itself in order. Rather, the methods I will discuss must be practiced and fine-tuned to help you succeed. In addition, everyone is different and who you are as a person will impact what methods work best for you. As you change and develop, you will need to refine these methods.

You need to think of this as a process and you are just starting out. So don't be too hard on yourself if you find it difficult at first.

Changes Worth Making

Let's get right to it, then! If we are going to change something, we need a reason for the change.

Let's look at a jet airplane to help us get this process started. It burns fuel to propel the airplane through the air. It also has a pilot who steers the aircraft in a particular direction. In the same way, we need fuel or motivation to propel ourselves toward our goals. In addition, we are the pilots choosing the direction to steer our lives.

The consequence of not having a defined direction is that you may have all the right techniques and motivation, but find yourself flying in circles.

3 - Do We Really Need Goals?

There is often a temptation to skip the goal setting part of this entire system. However, that will come with severe consequences. The best thing to do is:

- First figure out where you are heading

- Figure out what needs to be done to get there.

However, just figuring out where you want to go also requires you to figure out where you are. It is this very dynamic of back and forth between where you are now and where you want to go that will help you see the path to how to get there.

What's So Special About Lists?

By now, you may already be asking yourself, "What is the big deal about lists? After all, how can a list really make such a big difference?" Well, let me tell you, the difference between success and failure is completely dependent upon the use of PowerLists™.

As you go through this book, I am going to help you build your PowerLists™ and refine them so they will bring you closer each day to achieving your goal.

There are two types of PowerLists™ I explore in my books. This book is focused on your personal PowerLists™ that you will create in order to reach your goals. My other books are focused on PowerLists™ I have created from the best advice, research, and wisdom principles exploring different subjects in order to help you make the most out of your life.

Do I Need a Computer for the PowerLists™?

You might think you aren't good with technology or perhaps becoming good at computers is actually one of your goals. However, you can do each of these exercises with notecards and a pencil, although using a computer is ideal for sorting and reorganizing your lists.

To help you out, I am including an Excel spreadsheet template[4] . When I describe how to set up your spreadsheet,

[4]http://www.powerlists.org/B01L02

you can use a separate notecard for each line in the list. Then, you can sort the cards the way you can easily sort an Excel list.

4 - PowerList™ #1: Self-Assessment List

Back when I was in the Air Force going to survival and evasion school, we were taught that the first step in navigation was to assess where we were. This was best done by using our topographical map and looking into the distance at the nearby mountains.

We could triangulate our location on a given map by finding those same large geographical features, then measuring the angles between them and find ourselves on the map. Since the training involved evading people, all of our navigation was done after dark.

One night, we lost track of how many steps we had taken and were suddenly surrounded by multiple mountains that all looked similar and didn't match the map. We had walked a long way and were unsure where we were.

"Anyone can plot a course with a map or compass; but without a sense of who you are, you will never know if you're already home." - Shannon L. Alder

We can see that self-assessment plays a critical role in achieving our goal. However, all too often this step is skipped because we think we know where we are. In reality, we have often drifted off course and don't know where we are.

Where Are You?

Military training told us to stop everything and figure out where we were instead of walking off in any direction. Far too often people want to start something without taking a moment to assess their location.

For those who take the time, it is important to do an honest assessment. Often, we allow other people's opinions of us or our own opinions of ourselves to influence the quality of the assessment we take. The assessment can be too high or too low a view of ourselves.

Areas to Examine

Several areas are important to look at closely when doing a self-assessment:

- Physical health

- Mental health

- Spiritual well being

- Work life

- Family/Friends life

- Hobbies

- Financial situation

- Education

These items are not in any special order, and most likely

items could be added.

How Are You Doing?

Whatever the case, we need to examine these different items and ask ourselves how we are doing. By conducting this self-assessment we can lay the groundwork, and we can determine where we want to go now.

It is important to keep in mind that many times we are not in a good position to make a correct self-assessment. This is where a mentor or a close friend can help with the process.

The Influence of Other People, Part 1

Our self-assessment may be based upon people around us and our feelings about how different areas of *their* lives are going compared to *ours*. However, this may not be a good starting point when doing a self-assessment because the people around us may not have everything together in these areas. Comparisons can be dangerous.

There is also the issue that others may present only one side of themselves to the world. Other people may impose a standard on you which they themselves don't keep. Thus, it is important to remain true to your own standards.

Step Outside of Yourself

The key to examining yourself is to be neither too positive nor negative. Rather, try to remain neutral.

One trick to succeed is to imagine yourself as a doctor examining yourself as the patient. Your job is to assess where the patient is. This trick will enable you to be 100% honest with yourself. The tendency to lie to ourselves is often quite difficult to overcome.

This is where we bring other people into the picture. Perhaps you have a friend who can be honest with you. It is important to ensure that they give you an honest response. Avoid being defensive when they do an honest assessment of you.

Creating/Using PowerList™ #1: Self-Assessment List

Take a tab on a spreadsheet on your computer. At the top of each tab, label an area of your life you wish to work on. Underneath, label a column "Positives" on the left and "Negatives" on the right.

Next, fill out the positives and the negatives. Remember to be honest and try to give yourself a true assessment.

If you have a close friend or family member who will be honest with you, have them make the same assessment on you. This will be especially useful when you see differences between their assessment and yours.

Do not continue with this book until you have completed this step. Remember, the key difference between a normal list and a PowerList™ is precisely the fact that this list needs to be brutally honest. A failure to keep it honest will damage the other PowerLists™ we will discuss later in this book.

Finally, take each of these items on your spreadsheet and put them in order of what is most important for you to change. Sometimes we will see that the areas we thought we needed improvement on were fine and maybe better than we originally would have guessed.

Other times it may be the opposite. That is to say, we might think we are doing fine in an area when compared to people around us. After further examination of the Self-Assessment PowerList™, we realize that the negatives were much greater than we originally had considered. Thus, this assessment should move higher up the stack.

Whatever the case, you will find one of your self-assessments at the top of your stack. That will put you in a great position for the next step in the program.

Example

PowerList™ #1: Self-Assessment List	
General Health	

#	Positives	Negatives
1	Able to go on walks without losing breat	15 lbs. overweight
2	Muscles strong enough to do housework	Lack Energy
3	Good cholesterol count	Have difficulty sleeping
4	Get annual checkups	Rarely workout
5	Quit Smoking a year ago	High blood pressure
6		Eat junk food regularly
7		Use Facebook 3 hours a day
8		

Creativity		
#	Positives	Negatives
1	Practice doodling now and then	Always too busy to do hobbies
2	Write in a journal daily	Watch too much TV
3	Take photos with camera	Never take any courses
4	Play pretend with the kids	Never use paint brushes I own
5		Scared to show other people my work
6		
7		
8		

5 - PowerList™ #2: Goals List

When I transitioned from military life to a managerial role in the oil and gas services industry, I found that I was able to use the management skills that I had acquired.

However, deep down I saw that this wasn't where I wanted to be. I realized that if I were sick, I could easily be replaced in my job like a cog in a machine. I realized that I had skills that were much more powerful than managing people and resources. However, I simply hadn't taken the time to figure out what I was trying to achieve.

"Setting goals is the first step in turning the invisible into the visible." -Tony Robins

He is making a point here that we should remember. By setting goals, we also make the possibility of reaching them a reality. Without a goal, it is impossible to hit the target.

From Assessment to Goals

We can use our first PowerList™ from assessments and get

an idea of which goals will best address our top issue. There is no need to make any hard choices yet. Rather, you can ask yourself how achieving a particular goal would change the result for that self-assessment. This is a powerful way of seeing exactly what you need.

For example, if you assessed that you always show up late to appointments, you could create the goal of always being on time. Thus, if you achieved that goal, you would have a different assessment the next time around.

Notice we still aren't looking at how we reach a goal or even which goal we are shooting for. Rather, we are focusing on the connection between a negative assessment and the goal that would resolve that issue.

The Influence of Other People, Part 2

Establishing other people's goals for your life can be very disappointing.

Imagine reaching a goal only to discover it wasn't *your* goal. Rather, the goal belonged to someone else who had influence on you, and you realize that you adopted their vision as *your* vision. This is why you need to look deep into yourself and decide which goals are yours.

Seeing someone else get an aspect of their life together might have a huge impact on the choices you make regarding your goals. You wonder if you should work on the same goal. However, this can lead to your feeling hopeless because you are so different. One thing is clear: when someone pulls it together, it forces you to realize that it is doable; still, this may not be the top area for you to concentrate on.

Poor Goals

Another problem is having a goal that isn't concrete or easy to explain. Concrete goals are, for example, losing ten pounds or taking a class in photography. You need a time table. When exactly do you see yourself reaching this goal? It also needs to be measurable in the sense that once you have succeeded at reaching your goal, you should be able to check the item off as completed.

Too many people have goals that fail in this area. Their goals are abstract, unclear, and not related to a time frame. The result is that they never reach their goals; reaching the goal was impossible to identify since they never clearly defined what they were trying to achieve.

Creating/Using PowerList™ #2: Goals List

Now it's time to use your second PowerList™. This time we will make a list of all possible goals that we can generate.

You should notice that this list corresponds to your first PowerList™, your self-assessments. The next step is to order the list based on priority. Since you already have done this with your self-assessment list, your goal list may be in a similar order.

In addition, you may find that as you move through the different PowerLists™ you see that you didn't do a good job defining the previous list. In that case, go back and try again. You may see this play out in later lists. If you are unclear as to what you should include in your goal list, your self-assessment list probably needs more work.

We aren't looking for perfection here. However, the system requires enough work on each list so that when we reach the next list, it should flow easily from the previous list.

Now, take a deep breath and honestly ask yourself what area of your life you want to improve. We need to do some serious thinking about this. Also, you will find that your goals list is greatly influenced by your friends, family, and co-workers as your self-assessment is. Peer pressure to conform to a standard can be overwhelming.

This most important goal should be your top goal. This is where most people make a huge mistake. They attempt to achieve multiple goals at the same time. Instead, it is better to concentrate on the top item on your PowerList™. Shooting for more than one goal can easily derail your chances of reaching any of your goals.

SMART

When creating your goals list, it is helpful to look at the acronym SMART (from Aileen MacMillan, Performance Management Research Analyst):

- S - Specific

- M - Measurable

- A - Achievable/Attainable

- R - Results oriented/Realistic/Relevant

- T - Time Bound

This is helpful in determining the requirements for a well-defined goal.

Visualize Success

One other trick to help you select the right goal to work on first is to think about how it would feel if you achieved this goal. Imagine whatever goal you have chosen and now see yourself in the future having reached that goal. See the image in your head and ask yourself if it was worth the sacrifices you made to reach it. Are you happier? Is it like you thought it would be?

If you find it difficult to visualize what success feels like, you might have the wrong goal. Like running a marathon, you need to envision crossing the finish line and imagining how it will make you feel.

I don't have the same goal you do. Thus, when picturing myself crossing that line, it simply doesn't excite me at all. If you don't get excited about the image of crossing the finish line, it is a sign that you have chosen the wrong goal.

Your goal needs to be something you can envision having achieved and can imagine feeling great about. If not, then move this goal down on your list and try to find a different goal that you can clearly see yourself excited about reaching.

When we choose a goal that is too vague or undefined, it's hard to know if we have achieved it. It may be so diffuse that when we achieve it, we don't experience the rush that we ought to. Perhaps it is so unclear that we aren't sure if we have achieved it. This is a serious problem.

Example

PowerList™ #2: Goals List	
Rank	Goal
1	Lose 15 lb.
2	Work out at the gym 3 times a week
3	Complete an art course by the end of the year
4	Write a book in the next year
5	Start a blog in the next month
6	Travel to Rome in the next year
7	
8	
9	

6 - PowerList™ #3: Goal Road Map

After a decade of working as a manager, I discovered I enjoyed my side projects of building reports and analyzing data more than I enjoyed managing. I needed to find a goal that matched my personal abilities.

However, I couldn't go back to school and start over studying the subjects that would give me the skills I needed to reach this new goal. The path was murky and I wasn't even clear whether there was a path at all.

"A goal without a plan is just a wish." - Antoine de Saint-Exupéry

We can see there is a direct link between planning/road mapping and reaching our goal.

Where Do We Start?

At this point, you have now assessed where you are and

where you want to be heading. However, the path to get there isn't clear.

The next step is creating your goal road map. To accomplish anything, you need to select a path for how you are going to get there. This step needs to be clear and with time constraints similar to the goal itself. For example, if you want to write a book, you should decide how many words per day you need to write.

If you are starting a company, you need to decide how much research you will put into your business plan on a daily basis.

If you wish to lose weight, you need to decide how many calories per day you will eat and when you will exercise each day.

Break It Down!

When you are working toward a large goal, it is best to break it down into parts. Most goals can't be achieved with a single task. Therefore, if your goal is to build a house, you wouldn't have the first step be "build a house." Rather, you would need to buy land, make plans, hire an architect, secure proper funding and so on.

Some of these required tasks will be recurring and others will be one-time events.

Make Sure the Steps Aren't Fads

When looking at the single tasks that will get you to your goal, make sure they are based on science and not quack theories or the latest fads. This can be done by using respectable news outlets. They will give you information about research on that subject and give suggestions about how to break your goals down.

Steal From Other People

Don't get me wrong here; I'm not saying you should steal from other people. However, if someone has already invented the wheel and your goal is to build a car, don't reinvent the wheel. Instead, find someone who reached the same goal you are striving for. Learn what steps they used and modify their approach.

This idea is particularly important when you are trying to accomplish a large task and it isn't obvious how you should proceed. With the world interconnected as it is, you can always find people who have blogs and information about how to get to the place you are trying to reach. In addition, they have made mistakes and learned from them. Those people are key to your success.

Habits

Your road map should involve daily habits you will form in order to reach your goal. These will help you accomplish the recurring tasks, which are part of your goal road map. Your road map should be so clear that if you were able to follow through with this daily habit, you would surely reach your goal.

Phillippa Lally, a health psychology researcher at University College London, published a study[5] in the *European Journal of Social Psychology*. She noted that it takes more

[5]http://www.powerlists.org/B01L04

than two months to form a habit.

One-Time Tasks

One-time tasks will also be part of your road map. For example, you might get a membership at the local gym as part of your goal to lose weight. However, you can clearly see that this is where the habits come into play. What good is it to be a member of a gym unless you go to the gym regularly?

Creating/Using PowerList™ #3: Goal Road Map

We have the first two PowerLists™ under control at this point and are ready to create our PowerList™ #3 for our Goal Road Map.

This list should include steps necessary to complete your goal. This time, take your spreadsheet and fill out the necessary actions for reaching your goal. If they are recurring, mark how often they should recur. Recurring actions are the central part of making your goal a reality. One way to think

of the non-recurring actions is that they create the environment necessary for the recurring actions.

For example, buying a computer and some books on programming would be a single one-time action. However, in-
vesting 30 minutes a day in working through the book and
practicing programming would be a recurring item. You will
notice that the one-time event only created an environment
whereas the recurring task helps you reach your goal.

It is important to circle the recurring items since they are
most important. They will also be a core part of our next
chapter, which is about PowerList™ #4 Daily Checklist.

Two additional steps can be useful here when making your
road map. One is writing down how much time each task
will take. The other is keeping in mind the relationship
between the different tasks and their subtasks.

Being aware of how much time each task takes will be useful
when it comes to deciding when that task will be accomplished.

More importantly, being aware of the relationships between the tasks will help ensure you steadily achieve progress. Sometimes we make a list of things we need to get done. To bake a cake, we follow the recipe. If we get to a given point in the recipe and discover that we are missing something, we must decide to:

- Stop baking the cake

- Find alternative ingredients *or*

- Ask someone to go to the store *or*

- Move to a different step in the baking process that doesn't require the ingredient.

This interruption was triggered by not properly identifying at the beginning the one-time task of doing an inventory of necessary ingredients.

You might be tempted to stop making progress because you have hit a roadblock on one of your tasks. By knowing the interdependencies of the tasks, you are in a better position to navigate the challenges. Whatever you do, make sure that you keep moving toward your goal.

Action Alone Doesn't Count for Much If It Isn't Moving Toward a Goal

Another problem some people have is thinking they can skip the goal identification process and skip over to the daily and action lists. However, that is a huge mistake. Just because you are busy doing things doesn't mean you are doing the *right* things. In fact, it would be better to be less busy and actually be doing the things that are getting you closer to your goal.

Devoting time to unnecessary tasks takes important time away from the necessary things you ought to be concentrating on. So, do yourself a favor and make sure to have your goal in place with the road map before moving on.

See the Excel template[6] for an example of how to fill out the Goal Road Map for your goal. The key is to get the order

[6]http://www.powerlists.org/B01L02

right and identify which items are recurring versus single point events and also determine how much time each one will take. If an action will take fifty hours to complete, you might want to break it down into a recurring item daily for ten days at five hours per day.

This is because you won't be able to work for fifty hours straight to complete this item. However, if the item can be completed without disturbing your other recurring items, then it is wise to leave it as a single event.

Example

PowerList™ #3: Goal Road Map			
Order	ACTION	TIME NEEDED	RECURRING?
1	Sign up at gym	1 hour	-
2	Go to gym before work each day	1.5 hours	Daily
3	Download healthy recipes app	1 hour	-
4	Plan weeks healthy food	30 minutes	Sundays
5	Make Healthy food	1 hour	Daily
6	Check weight	5 minutes	Daily
7	Go to bed by 10PM	1 minute	Daily
8	Watch only 1 hour of TV	1 hour	Daily
9	Sit in front of computer only 30 minutes	30 minutes	Daily
10	Find accountability partner	1 hour	-
11	Check in with accountability partner	10 minutes	Sundays
12			
13			

7 - PowerList™ #4 Daily Checklist

Every morning, I found I would forget something important. I would be heading off to work only to discover I had
forgotten my telephone or another important item. Sometimes I would head back home to get it and wonder how I
could have forgotten it. Other times, I would start the day
by seeing an e-mail in my inbox and taking time to give a
long reply.

Then, I would notice the clock, see it was time to go and
realize I hadn't gotten my coffee or done the other important tasks. I tried to remember everything I needed to do, including the simple stuff. It wasn't working. No matter what
I intended, there were either things I forgot or I got distrac-
ted by things that lured me away and got me off track.
Something was missing.

"One way to meet your goals is to keep a daily task list. This
is a handy trick borrowed from the most successful business
leaders. Sometimes important deadlines sneak up on us and
take us by surprise, so we end up trying to do too many

things at the last minute." - Grace Fleming, [7] "How To Meet Goals With a Daily Task List", *About Education*

This is an extremely important point since we are better prepared to achieve our goals if we break them down into small but doable daily tasks.

The Most Important Brick

The daily checklist is the most important part of the entire goal achievement process. There is no other single thing I could recommend to help you pull aspects of your life together and reach your goal.

We already have identified where we are, where we are heading, and what it will take to get there.

However, this is only the beginning. PowerList™ #4 Daily Checklist is the motor that will make this happen.

People who follow a daily checklist are much more likely to achieve their long-term goal.

[7] http://www.powerlists.org/B01L05

In reality, everyone has a daily checklist. Perhaps, it is only in their heads and not on paper or in a spreadsheet. That is where the first problem starts. When we keep something in our head, there is a tendency to forget and fall back into previous habits regarding time management.

This Is Your Time Budget

A budget is simply a plan for spending your money. Your daily checklist is a time budget. It is a plan for spending your time. It starts as an honest assessment of how you are currently spending your time. After a great deal of refinement, it will begin to reflect how you wish to spend your time and will slowly shape your actions toward the way you ought to spend your time.

Creating/Using PowerList™ #4: Daily Checklist

Look at the Excel template[8] included with this book for an idea of how to create your daily checklist.

---

[8]http://www.powerlists.org/B01L02

Start by writing down step-by-step everything you do throughout the day. I mean *everything* you do on a daily basis. This includes watching TV and using social media.

At this point, I want you to see which aspects of your daily routine could be cut out. You may be unaware of why many items are included in your daily routine. They have become habits.

Now you need to modify your daily list of actions and delete the items that aren't important. They can be neutral items, but they don't contribute to achieving your goals.

With extra space on your PowerList™, you can add items to your daily list that you had on your previous list under re-curring tasks.

You will want to add these items as early in the day as possible. This is because the brain works best early in the day when it is freshest. Later in the day you will be tired and it will be easier to skip these steps.

Once complete, you should have a large list of all the things you plan to do each day. Hopefully, every item on the list is necessary. By simply adding check boxes next to your list, you can mark off each item as the day starts until it ends.

As you complete these items, you can always reward yourself with one of the other items you removed from your daily list. You are now bringing your schedule into alignment with your goal.

How to Use Your List

Now, let's get into how to use this list. This list will determine the flow of what you do on a daily basis or what you *ought* to do on a daily basis. When you get up in the morning, perhaps you use the restroom and afterwards are tempted to start your daily routine. That might include getting coffee, reading the news, or going onto social media. However, that is about to change.

From this point on, you will wake up and you will go straight to your list before doing anything else. In fact, your list will include things like getting coffee, brushing your teeth, showering, and other essential things. You will now follow your list in the exact order that it is written and you won't deviate from the list until the entire list is complete.

You will want to ensure fun things are on the list. However, remember that going through a set of routines without analyzing whether they are getting you closer to your goal will always result in your choosing the path of least resistance. This includes making choices that waste your time and perhaps even move you further from your goal. This is why you need to follow this list exactly as written.

Fix Your List Continually

As you start using your daily list, you will find problems. Perhaps you forgot items So you will add them to your list. Or perhaps you will see that some items are a waste of time. These items should be removed.

Additionally, you may find your list is so long that no matter how hard you work during the day, you never get to the end of it. Keep in mind that we already established that the list is what you actually do on a daily basis.

Given perfect conditions, you should be able to complete all items on your list. If that isn't happening, then your list isn't reflecting what you actually do.

At the same time, if you find you are able to complete the entire list early in the day, then it is time to add items. You will be doing something later in the evening. These items should be on the list; even if it is sitting in front of a TV for 4 hours, it should be added to your list. You are filling your day with something even if it is staring out the window or sleeping in bed. So, make sure you add everything to your list.

As I mentioned earlier, this is a time budget. When budgeting your money, every penny should be accounted for. If money is left over it should go to savings or be used for something fun (since you have done a great job following your budget). Whatever the case, all your time and money should be accounted for.

One powerful thing about this list is that it will honestly show you how you are spending your time. When you look at your time usage, it makes you ask yourself whether you are happy with your choices.

If you aren't, then this is a perfect chance to work on it. Simply change the items around until you see this list reflect how you want to spend your time (that is, in a way that is working toward your goal and not away from it).

Where the Rubber Meets the Road

The final and most important part of the PowerList™ #4 is following it. That means when you wake up every morning, you need to open the daily list and start going through it item by item. If the order is wrong or the list needs correction, then make the changes.

The final task each day is to ask yourself whether this list is being followed. Not following your list will seriously decrease your chances of achieving your long-term goal. You have to decide whether you are serious about reaching your goal.

As a final reminder, your PowerList™ #4 is the most important part of the entire system. It creates the habits that will lead to your success. If you fail at getting this PowerList™ in place, you will find that the other parts of this system will be of little help to you. This list also happens to be the one least used by people.

Getting control over your PowerList™ #4 can compensate for failure anywhere else or in any of the other lists. That is to say, if you are regularly looking at what you are doing on a daily basis, wasted time will be visible to you and should trigger a change in your PowerList™ #4.

Example

PowerList™ #4 Daily Checklist	
Order	ACTION
1	Wake up
2	Brush Teeth
3	Brush Hair
4	Get dressed
5	Get coffee
6	Eat breakfast
7	Check Task Management List for the day
8	Check e-mail
9	Check social media
10	Make lunch
11	Pack workbag
12	Drive to gym
13	Shower
14	Drive to work
15	Drive Home
16	Make Dinner
17	Do daily items in task management list for the day
18	Adjust Task Management List for upcoming days
19	Watch TV
20	Use social Media
21	Go to sleep

8 - PowerList™ #5: Task Management List

We cleaned the house regularly, but there was always deep cleaning that we never had time for. Something as simple as cleaning underneath the refrigerator or dusting never seemed to fit into the schedule. In all, we realized that there were 45 tasks that did not get completed during a 6-month period.

However, it was simply not possible to keep this information in our heads. Sometimes, we would try marathon cleaning. However, burnout hit quickly. We clearly needed a better system for keeping track of what had been done and which tasks were coming up next. The lack of some sort of system guaranteed that we would have chaos.

"Having a good task management system--a list of tasks with a process for maintaining it--is important for being to be productive. The main benefit here is that you get all your tasks out of your head.

This means you feel more relaxed and can concentrate more easily, knowing that you haven't missed anything. Capturing all your tasks also makes you less likely to miss something important." - Richard Batty, "<u>Dramatically increase your productivity by using a task management system</u>"[9] , *80000 Hours*

I can't agree more with Richard. A well-developed task management system reduces stress and ensures a better way of handling the mountain of tasks needed to reach your goal.

What Is It?

The task management system is the place where you focus on the single event task or the recurring events that aren't happening on a daily basis.

As we mentioned before, the real meat of reaching your goal is what you do on a daily basis. However, it is these single-event tasks or long-term, recurring items that create the environment for success.

[9]http://www.powerlists.org/B01L06

Examples of long-term recurring events are paying your gym membership fee every six months or going to the doctor for your annual checkup. However, it really depends upon which goal you are trying to achieve.

You Already Have This

In reality, you have these lists already. Perhaps you simply are holding them in your head. Or, maybe they are on scraps of paper.

Bills in the Drawer

Another popular place to keep tasks is in the same format you receive them. For example, if you receive mail telling you to pay your electricity bill or to renew your membership, you have a piece of paper that tells you the task. You might put those papers in a drawer.

However, you still have to remember to go back to them. In addition, while the papers contain the dates by which you need to take action, there is no trigger to get you to act on these dates. As you can see, keeping these papers in the drawer does not solve your problem.

E-Mail

In the digital world, e-mail is a major source of notifications for things we need to do. Since they are in writing, people often assume that these tasks are already in a good task management system. After all, with e-mail, they are quickly sorted by date and even by sender. However, they don't tell you when you need to take the next action.

E-mail is a poor system for task management. The problem is that the e-mails are clustered and even if you put them in special folders for each type of task or category, you still have to mentally keep track of when you will take action.

You can read more about how to manage your e-mail in my free e-book here[10] .

Phone Calls, Conversations and Ideas

We interact with people throughout the day. Many times,

[10]http://www.powerlists.org/s9si

we will hear something or be saying something that reminds us of something we need to do. Where exactly are we storing all of these tasks? The answer for most of us is in our heads.

What's Wrong with Using Your Head?

The answer to this is very simple: everything! In fact, your head is a lousy place to store critical information that you need to achieve your goal. This might be possible if the only thing you were trying to focus on was achieving your goal.

However, your head is filled with many things related to family, work, and miscellaneous notions. This is where the PowerList™ #4 Daily Checklist and PowerList™ #5 are so important.

What Should the PowerList™ #5 include?

The task list should include everything you need or want to remember to do. In fact, there should not be anything you wish or need to remember that is excluded from your task system.

Impact of a Task Management List

The benefits of a task list system are enormous. It is worth taking time to review the immediate benefits of using this powerful tool.

Stress Reduction

The first thing most people notice when implementing a task list is that their stress levels go down. There is no fear of forgetting something. The important thing is to update it continually.

What can you forget if everything is written down?

Perfect for Planning

A task list gives you an excellent area for planning. You can quickly see what you need to do and as long as it is prioritized and has due dates attached, you can swap items around to space out exactly when you plan to work these different issues.

History of Accomplishments

This particular point is especially important for two reasons. The first and most important impact is the psychological impact of being able to cross items off your list and feel you are getting things done.

All too often people believe they are working and yet never get anything done. This is false. You are, in fact, doing something even if it is cleaning or watching TV. The beauty of using a system like this is that you can document that you aren't just getting things done. Rather you are getting *specific* things done that are directly connected to your goal.

The second aspect of the history of accomplishments is that you can use this when building up your resume or applying for a job. If these tasks are work related, you will have specific documentation for what you have accomplished and when. This is also helpful when completing job performance reviews.

Creating/Using PowerList™ #5: Task Management System

Now you may wonder what the tool looks like. Let me break it down for you. At its most basic level it is a simple list of tasks. Each item has a task, date for next action, priority, time required, due date, actions taken, and recurrence pattern. When you complete an action, you fill out the action taken area.

If you run out of space, you can create a new task to split this task in two. I like to include dates in front of each action taken so I can see my progress on a given task. Then, you simply put a date completed next to each item you have completed.

At this point, I highly recommend you use a digital task management system such as Tasks in Microsoft Outlook or a spreadsheet like the one included with this book.

A quick Google search reveals 327,000 hits for "Task Management System." So, there is no lack of software available.

My task system has evolved over the years. In the beginning, I used Microsoft Outlook Tasks. I then moved from Tasks to Excel and when it was overloaded, I moved to MS Access.

Using a spreadsheet is important here since you will need to sort your list by priority and then by the due date. This will then give you the order of the tasks. For any given day, you simply ensure the top priority items come first.

Then, when you complete a given task, you remove it from the list and move it to a separate spreadsheet for competed tasks. It is important to regularly keep your eye on how many tasks you have completed. This will build your sense of getting something done.

I paste the header data from e-mails under each task in Excel. This makes it possible to find relevant e-mails later. I also include a short comment on what the e-mail says. This makes it possible to come back to a given issue and look up the relevant e-mails to track the progress of a given task.

Much of this exercise is dealing with psychological barriers to success. When you see all of the work you are doing, it builds a mental image that you are the type of person who gets things done. After all, just look at the list in front of you for what you have accomplished today.

Finally, mark recurring tasks so that you know you will never finish that task, but will rather do it again at a set time. Then, mark it as completed and set a new due date based upon the time you need to do it again.

Example

DUE DATE	TASK	ACTIONS TAKEN	TIME REQUIRED	PRIORITY	RECURRENCE PATTERN	DATE COMPLETED
		PowerList™ #5: Task Management List				
15.Oct.2014	Sign up at gym	Dropped by the local gym and signed up for 6 months	1 hour	High	-	12.oct.2014
16.Oct.2014	Download healthy recipes app	Found app with shopping list and recipes	1 hour	Medium	-	16.Oct.2014
17.Oct.2014	Plan weeks healthy food	Used planner function on app to plan out meals	30 minutes	Medium	Sundays	17.Oct.2014
18.Oct.2014	Find accountability partner		1 hour	High	-	
24.Oct.2014	Check in with accountability partner		10 minutes	High	Sundays	

9 - The Calendar

I recently started understanding how powerful a digital calendar can be. I had tons of things I wanted to do and I thought it was just a matter of scheduling them on my calendar. So, I started at first with one item per half hour. I then filled up my calendar with all of the things I wanted to accomplish. I quickly noticed that if too many items were on a given line, it was hard to read.

So, I spaced them out to ensure there were no more than four items for a given half-hour block. Now, I was ready to get these tasks done and to reach my different goals. Except for one problem: simply putting items on the calendar didn't mean that other demands for that same time would go away. Thus, I may have erased a couple of the completed tasks from the calendar.

However, I still had a hundred items. So, the next day started and I dragged and dropped each item from the previous day to the next day. I had come up with a few new items to fit on the calendar. One of them would go to 5 AM and the other to midnight.

It was not possible to read them if there were more than four items per half-hour block. I continued this process until I realized a calendar makes a lousy task management system. I also lost the sense of empowerment I originally had and was left helpless. There had to be a better way.

"This seems so simple, but it is amazing how much a calendar can change your life! . . . By using a calendar, you allow yourself to stay focused, motivated, and disciplined towards reaching your goals. You also learn to take responsibility for important actions that need to be done." - Maristella Bacod-Gebhardt, Counselor, "How to use a calendar effectively!"[11] , *Sacramento City College*

This is why we don't want to skip over this commonly used but often misunderstood tool.

What the Calendar Is Not

I want to get this out of the way. The calendar is not your task management system. This is so important I need to say it again. The calendar is not your task management system!

[11]http://www.powerlists.org/B01L07

Many people have no other task management system so they think that filling up their calendar with all of the things they need to do will help get them done.

Let me comment that I fell into this trap a decade or so ago. The way you know you have gone down the wrong path is when you find yourself with a calendar that is packed with lots of things to do but at the end of each day, you drag them over to the next day and pile them on top of another pile for tomorrow.

Now that we've gotten that out of the way, let's take a closer look at what the calendar is.

Correct Use of the Calendar

The calendar should be a place to store tasks that you will do during your day. This may include meetings, single tasks or recurring actions.

Mark on your calendar the time when you will start your daily checklist. Your daily checklist will tell you when you need to start your action list in your task management system. You also can place specific actions from your action list on your calendar if you have time for them and will be able to get them accomplished.

Your calendar is where meetings will be registered; there will also be reminders as to when you need to drop off the kids, get the mail, or anything that you not only wish to do, but *will* do. *All optional issues should be left off your calendar.*

Your calendar should also be linked to your smart phone so you always have it with you. It should beep a reasonable amount of time before each item to give you fair notice of upcoming tasks. In addition, you need to train yourself to follow your calendar exactly. When you ignore its beeping, your calendar's usefulness deteriorates.

Reminders and Keeping It All Together

With your calendar in place, you no longer have to store events in your head. Rather, events are in writing and even recurring events are registered. This will give you fewer things to think about. After all, you are trying to achieve your goal and you want your mind and emotions focused on reaching it.

You don't need the stress of being concerned about events that may happen. Rather, any event you have should be registered on your calendar. Any normal daily routine will be registered in your daily list and all non-daily items will be registered in your task management system. This keeps it clear as to what goes where.

10 - PowerList™ #6: Motivations List

I found myself going to bed later and later than I wanted to each night. I knew that sleep plays a vital role in health and keeping a clear mind. So, I was convinced that I ought to be sleeping more.

Yet, when it came time to go to bed each night, there were too many things I needed to do. Additionally, I wanted to watch TV or use social media. What was I missing? Why wasn't I doing the very thing that I knew was good for me and that I wanted to do?

"When it comes to cultivating genius, talent matters, but motivation may matter more." - Daisy Yuhas, "Three Critical Elements Sustain Motivation"[12] , *Scientific American*

Thus, it is worth taking time to look at our motivation.

---

[12]http://www.powerlists.org/B01L08

Tricks for Keeping It Going

Motivation is a tricky yet important thing. It is the fuel that keeps us moving. Like a rocket that is powered by solid fuel, motivation is required for us to achieve our goals.

When we start any project, we experience a burst of energy and direction. We experience a pull and a push perhaps at the same time. The pull is the alluring nature of a new project to achieve our goal and the push is knowing we aren't there yet and need to get moving.

If we were able to sustain this level of motivation throughout the project, some of our lists would perhaps become less relevant. However, we will see the motivation increase and decrease throughout the project. Thus, we need to use tricks to keep our actions in line with our goals.

Now, I want to explore several tricks.

Pomodoros

The word *pomodoro* comes from the Italian word for tomato. In particular, pomodoro is a tomato-shaped timer that ticks as the minutes are being counted down. The idea behind this method, originated in the early 1980s by Francesco Cirillo, is that blocking off time into focused uninterrupted blocks is the best way to work.

The alternative is to work only when we are motivated and stop when we lose motivation. The problem with this second method is that we tend to lose motivation quickly and our lack of productivity leads to even more loss of productivity. After all, we are creatures of habit.

When we practice not working toward our goal, we tend to keep moving in accordance with that lack of productivity. It is important to block off chunks of time to ensure that we develop a habit of being productive, whether we want to or not.

So, how does this method work? It's simple: you work for 25 minutes, take a 25 minute break and then repeat this pattern four times. After that, you take a 30-minute break and continue the cycle again.

This can be done with the help of the dozens of apps for your iPhone or Android. I personally like <u>Flat Tomato</u>[13] on my iPhone and am even using it now to write this book.

Remember that you need to put your phone in airplane mode and exit your e-mail and social media in order to focus on a single task.

One of the main ideas behind this trick is that we are terrible at multitasking and, unlike many other skills, the more we multitask the worse we get.

Try this method. Perhaps it will work for you as it has for thousands of other people. By blocking off chunks of time, you will find your motivation to work increases as you see your work getting done and you move closer to your goal one pomodoro at a time.

Accountability

Another trick is to stay motivated by having another person hold you accountable. The key here is that when other

[13]http://www.powerlists.org/B01L09

people are aware of your trying to achieve your goal, they check up on how you are doing.

Knowing that someone will ask you how your tasks are coming along can push you to work harder. For example, you might see this occur at the gym. Simply having other people present can cause you to work harder. After all, you don't want others to see you slacking off when they are working hard.

Consequences Are Your Friends

There is another commonly practiced trick, which is to set up consequences. If you want to ensure that you achieve your goal, you can set up positive and negative consequences to motivate yourself.

On the positive side of things, you can give yourself a reward when you reach certain milestones or you manage to keep doing your daily tasks for a specific period of time. These rewards can also be set up automatically through websites like stickK[14] and Beeminder[15] that take a certain amount of money from you and then give it back to you once you have achieved a milestone.

In addition, there are negative ways of doing this, which involves giving someone or certain websites a certain amount of money in a type of escrow account. The other party is authorized to keep the money if you don't reach your goal.

Another twisted version of this involves websites where money that you have put in escrow will be transferred to organizations you dislike if you fail to reach your goal. The negative motivation can often be more effective than positive motivation.

Others on the Same Path

Another strategy for motivation is to find other people who are on the same path as you are, trying to achieve the same goal. When you need a little extra encouragement, they are able to give it.

[14]http://www.powerlists.org/B01L10
[15]http://www.powerlists.org/B01L10

We are more influenced by the people around us than many of us are aware.

Don't Break the Chain

This method is often attributed to the TV series Seinfeld. The idea is very simple. Set up a small calendar and put an X on each day you do the tasks necessary to achieve your goal. After a number of days, you will start to notice the formation of a chain. Then, you have a new goal, which is to "not break the chain." Keep it going as long as possible and do absolutely everything to ensure the chain keeps growing.

A visual reminder of success and failure may be what you need to stay motivated. Even this very book was written using the chain method.

More information on this method can be found on Lifehacker.com[16] who credit Brad Isaac[17] for the idea.

---

[16]http://www.powerlists.org/B01L12
[17]http://www.powerlists.org/B01L13

Creating/Using PowerList™ #6: Motivations Lists

This PowerList™ is all about making a list of what motivates you to follow your daily checklist, your task management system and calendar. Notice that I am not asking you to look at what motivates you to achieve your goal.

This is because a failure to achieve your goal can always be traced to a failure to follow through with the previous PowerList™. You can see an example of how to set up this list in the Excel template[18] .

Identifying the things that work to motivate us is the key to tapping into that fuel that we can use when times get tough and we no longer have the desire to follow through with our plan.

This PowerList™ will look different for different people. For some, it might include positive and negative rewards and punishments. For others, it might be recognition of success or fear of embarrassment from failure.

[18]http://www.powerlists.org/B01L02

It might be tempting to skip over this list since it isn't the most important of the lists. However, it plays a key role when you want to give up. By looking at this list, we can see what we have or have not been using to keep us moving forward with our plan.

If we are going to fail, let's make sure it wasn't because we hadn't tried all of the tricks available to increase our motivation. Often, our failure is due to the part of us that tells us to give up and undermines the reasons we are trying to achieve this goal in the first place.

Once you have completed this list, you are free to move on to the next section. However, keep this list handy when you find yourself in a low motivation period.

You have no chance of succeeding if you are not motivated. You won't be motivated if you haven't bothered to figure out where that motivation comes from and how to get it to work for you.

Example

PowerList™ #6: Motivations List	
#	Positive	Negative
1	Pomodoros	Make deal to pay friend if I don't lose the weight in 6 months
2	Allowed to eat desert on Saturday if routine followed	
3	Find online forum of others using same strategies	
4	Avoid people who discourage reaching goal	
5	Set up don't break the chain calendar	
6		
7		
8		

68

11 - PowerList™ #7: Barriers List

I was 40 pounds (18kg) over my ideal weight. I knew that I ought to lose weight, but how exactly could I lose so much? It seemed like a mountain I would have to climb. Wouldn't I slide back anyway if I reached it? I had many friends who had lost weight only to gain it back in short order.

In addition, I had heard that if you start eating less food, the body simply responds by lowering your metabolism, which results in your gaining even more weight. What is the point in eating less if your body would simply compensate by going into a slow burning mode? It was clear that there were too many barriers to succeed at this goal. Or were there?

"It struck me at this moment, that many of our natural tendencies as humans actually hurt our chances of success, rather than helping them. Learning to move beyond the emotions that hold us back is tremendously important in our own quest for success." - Garrett Moon, "7 Barriers To Overcome For Success"[19] , *todaymade*

[19]http://www.powerlists.org/B01L14

Garrett is saying that there are a number of things that come naturally and create barriers to our success.

Road Blocks to Watch Out for

There are many barriers to success which you need to look at. These will get in the way of your reaching your goal. In particular, they will attack your forward progress. Thus, they should be watched closely to ensure you keep making progress.

Sabotage from Within

One issue that arises is the internal voice that tells us we aren't able to achieve this goal. It might tell us we aren't good enough, smart enough or fit enough. That voice can even sabotage our ability to follow our checklists. After all, since we know we won't ever be able to learn that new language or get a promotion, why should we try?

This voice inside can be a huge barrier. Therefore, it is important to be honest with ourselves. At the same time, realize that there are many difficult things that are within our reach if we have a plan.

Sabotage from Without

Perhaps our issue is coming from outside of ourselves. It could be that others are telling us that we can't accomplish our goals or they are even ridiculing our attempts to try. One reason people do this is because they wish they were the ones with the goals and an action plan. When they see someone making progress in an area that they struggle with, they really don't wish the best for that person.

Your ability to learn a new skill can be a threat to other people. It proves that you can change, learn, and grow, that you can achieve. Perhaps this is a contrast with other people in terms of what they did or didn't do or what they told themselves was impossible. Yet, there you are trying to achieve that very thing.

It isn't easy watching other people achieve their dreams when we have failed to achieve ours.

The key to dealing with people like this is to encourage

them. Let them know it wasn't as hard as it originally seemed as long as you have a system you are following. In addition, there is no need to rub their noses in your success. Rather, be honest with them about the struggles you faced.

Finally, if they continue to be hostile, it is best to put distance between you and them. Remember, they aren't a charity project. You must decide who you will spend time with. Also, don't underestimate the power of someone else to destroy your ability to make the changes needed to achieve your goals.

Burnout

Another issue to watch out for is that of being over-motivated. This is a very interesting problem because if we feel extremely high levels of motivation, it pushes us to work harder. However, there are two big issues that lead you to burnout or breaking your routines.

The first issue is that you decide instead of working for the planned amount of time you dedicated to achieving your goal, you put in five to ten times the amount of time. At one level, you might think it is a positive thing to invest ten hours in your work.

The problem is that after working so long, you begin to lose interest in the subject. You may find the energy you would naturally have had the next day will not be there when you try to work again.

Also, you may rate a normal day's work as not so good since you aren't as motivated the next day. Thus, you have raised the bar on what you consider a successful day of work. As a result, you may quickly find yourself burning out.

For example, you can see this if you are eager to hit the gym only to find that after going three hours at a time every day for a week, you stop going. A much better solution is to find the amount of work that is best for you that won't steal your motivation from the next day.

Urgent Versus Important

Other barriers can be things that are pressing and *feel* urgent. Notice I didn't say these things *are* urgent, but rather they *feel* urgent. In fact, many of them are not important at all, but trick us into devoting our time and energy as opposed to working on things that matter.

This is why the daily checklist is so important. It keeps you on track. Unless something is urgent and important, it must wait. It simply should not be given your focus and attention. It will try to trick you with the excitement around it and other people may try to raise its level of importance, but it is best to simply let it sit there until you have achieved the truly important things on your daily schedule.

Another trick to dealing with barriers is to just say no. Make a list of every time you say no. This will be your No List. After a while, you will begin to see that saying no isn't as difficult as you thought.

You are on your way to achieving a goal and you aren't going to let things that don't matter get in the way. A good way of looking at this is that saying "no" in one area of your life is actually saying "yes" somewhere else. Let's reserve a "yes" for something important like reaching a goal.

Work Bank?

The second issue is that you might look at all the work you did the first day as an excuse for not working so hard the next day. In fact, there is a tendency to think that you somehow have a bank of work and that if you do a lot of work today, then doing very little tomorrow should be acceptable. This line of reasoning is bankrupt.

Let's assume you will be away from your office or unable to work on your goal. You should not try to get extra work in since there will be a break. Instead, you need to simply follow your planned routine and do only the work that is scheduled.

You have only so much energy and only so much creative juice. Don't waste either. Rather, figure out the optimal amount of work for a given day and never exceed that amount.

The only exception to this rule is if you find that you are unable to be creative every day in the designated time. Then, if you get on a roll, you should keep going. If the quantity of the work being produced is taking a beating because of this strategy, you need to consider forcing yourself to work within time constraints every day whether you feel creative or not.

You can learn to adjust and create in chunks even if it doesn't come naturally at first. Keeping track of sporadic creativity is the key here.

Myths

Perhaps you have heard an old wives' tale regarding something, and you allowed this to influence whether you achieve your goal. For example, I believed that eating less would drop my metabolism so that my body would simply quit burning fat. That may be true to a limited degree.

However, the reality is that the body must burn something to survive. As long as you are staying active, the body will continue to burn whatever it can get its hands on. If you aren't giving it a lot of energy, then it resorts to burning the fat reserves that you already have. There is no such thing as activity without energy to support that activity.

The myth of metabolism is one of the reasons so many fad diets are popular. Many claim that you don't need to decrease consumption, but simply change what you eat and that will make the difference. Then you can eat as much as you want without any problem.

Once I read more on the subject, it occurred to me that a car that is moving will burn gas. Even if it is burning less gas at certain speeds, it is still burning fuel. It simply doesn't drive for free. So, overcoming this barrier is best done by using science; explore the research that has been conducted on this issue.

The worst part of myths is that they make us believe that the correct path isn't going to work. Even worse, they give us alternative solutions that have not been tested by science. Overly enthusiastic people sell these ideas to us and make piles of money with the latest techniques that simply do not work.

Procrastination

Another common barrier is procrastination. The PowerLists™ themselves are especially effective in dealing with this issue. In particular, your daily checklist should determine the order of events.

Your most important tasks are at the beginning of your list and you simply need to follow the checklist. Procrastination isn't necessarily the idea of doing something another day, in a few weeks or "later." Rather, it can also include saying you will do something later than planned.

When this occurs, you are doing several things that break the system. The first is that you aren't following your daily list. It was made when you weren't actually doing those tasks. Thus, you are letting your emotions or lack of motivation get in the way of determining what is important to you.

The second issue here is that you use up all of your best mental energy towards the beginning of the day. Therefore, you delay the tasks that are the most important until the end of the day when you are tired.

Finally and perhaps most importantly, putting something off until the end of the day increases the chances of you're not doing that task. If that occurs a number of times, a new habit is born and your productivity tanks until your entire goal achievement process falls apart completely.

So, do yourself a favor and follow your daily checklist. If it isn't optimized with your actual priorities, then fix it and follow the new order. Your calendar should tell you to open it each day and you need to do precisely that. Do not deviate from this list unless there is an emergency.

Mount Everest

This barrier usually hits you in the beginning of your journey to achieve your goal when you look at what you are trying to do and see that it looks like an enormous mountain. You can see the peak, but you are sure you will never be able to reach it.

You can overcome this barrier by asking yourself whether you have broken down your goal properly and, whether you will actually reach your goal if you follow your road map. If not, then you need to go back to the earlier PowerList™ and fix it until it shows a clear path to achieving your goal.

It is extremely important that you are convinced that your task list and your daily list are correct. If so, you should see that if you follow your lists, you will reach your goal. If you aren't convinced, then your lists aren't good enough.

Once you are convinced, then you need to remind yourself that you followed today's lists. You are on the correct path even if the goal itself seems too large.

It is also important to look at other people who have succeeded in climbing that mountain. No matter what your goal is, there are people who have also accomplished that goal. You need to convince yourself that they are like you. Some of them may have thought it wasn't possible until they accomplished it.

True Versus False Barriers

Some barriers simply can't be broken down or even gone around. For example, it may be common to tell children that they can go to the moon or be president if they try hard enough. That may be true for some, but for the vast majority it is a goal that has so many barriers that we must be

honest with ourselves regarding what is most likely to occur.

We are talking about true barriers. I don't want to discour-
age you from moving toward your goal. However, it is better
to shoot for something that you can, in fact, achieve. Goals
that are too high will demotivate you.

So instead of aiming to become an astronaut or president,
you could start by aiming to become a pilot, engineer, or
doctor if you want to be an astronaut, or go into local and
state politics if you want to become president. Don't set
goals that are not likely to be achieved. They do more harm
than good.

False barriers may seem true. So it is important to discern
which barriers are real barriers for you and which ones are
false. Ask others for help.

Creating/Using PowerList™ #7: Barriers List

Take out your spreadsheet and start building a list of which barriers are the biggest for you. For each item you need to write the name of the barrier, the description, consequences of giving in, and tricks to overcoming it. Order these items in terms of which barriers are most likely to derail your progress in reaching your goal.

The process of making these lists alone will help clarify areas where you need to stay vigilant. As the ancient Chinese General Sun Tzu said in *The Art of War*[20] , "Know your enemy and know yourself." This needs to be considered if you are going to succeed at reaching your goal. These barriers are your enemy. The order of this list isn't constant. It will continually change over time as you change.

For example, the goal of exercising every morning will have barriers that may include being too tired to get up, feeling soreness from the day before, or having too many other things you need to do, whereas studying for an online degree has a completely different set of challenges which don't involve physical pain.

Goals are easier when outside forces are pushing you to suc-

[20]http://www.powerlists.org/B01L15

ceed. That would be the case if you were a football player and morning exercises were essential. A different situation completely changes the barriers that will be in front of you.

Example

#	Name	Description	Consequence of Giving in	Tricks to overcoming
			PowerList™ #7: Barriers List	
1	Mount Everest	I feel that this goal is too big to reach	I won't reach the goal	Remind myself that Goal Roadmap is correct. I just need to follow through on daily checklist
2	Procrastination	I feel that I want to do the most important items at the end of the day	I will be too tired and lack motivation at end of day	Ensure daily checklist has these items at beginning of day and don't deviate
3	Burnout	I am tempted to do extra work outs since I feel plenty of energy.	I will lose motivation the following day to keep going	Ensure you do only what you planned and follow through with daily checklist.
4				
5				
6				
7				
8				

12 - PowerList™ #8: Evaluation List

After several years, I found myself doing what I loved best. I was working in system development and analysis, steering other development teams, and spending 95% of my time on tasks I enjoyed and found challenging. I had reached my goal. Or had I?

Simply being content with a given situation isn't enough. I hadn't assessed whether or not I had reached my goal. Even worse, it wasn't clear whether my goal was defined in the first place. Perhaps I just stumbled upon a situation that worked well for me. Wasn't it enough that I was happy with the situation?

Is it really worth the trouble of evaluating what happened?

"Reflection is something we don't usually allow ourselves to experience because we are too busy getting on to the next task at hand, too busy hurrying to the next assignment that we don't pay attention fully to what we have created in the last assignment, too busy grappling with the next hurdle because it is there rather than analyzing why we felt a certain way about our work just completed." - Mel Bost, "<u>Why is 'Reflection' So Important to Project Lessons Learned?</u>"[21] , of *ProjectSmart*

It is clear that reflection/evaluation play an important role in learning from our efforts to reach a goal.

Did We Achieve Our Goals?

Since we took the time needed on our second PowerList™ to ensure that our goals were well defined, it should be easy at this point to see if we did indeed achieve our goals.

If a goal was not clearly defined or perhaps lacked a deadline, it is possible that we reached this point in our project and are unsure of whether we met it or not. If that is the case, then it is clear we need to start the process over again.

However, perhaps you did, in fact, achieve the very thing that you wanted to achieve. This is a time for celebration.

[21]http://www.powerlists.org/B01L16

You should be proud of yourself. By using the different PowerLists™ in the way they were intended to be used, you reached your goal and now it is time to start the process over again with a new goal.

An important thing to remember here is that if you reached your goal, you may still need to keep some of your tasks in place in order to sustain the goal. For example, did you lose the weight you wanted, run the marathon or learn a new skill?

If so, you still may need to work to keep your skills or physical fitness at the level you achieved. You must remember that it only takes abandoning your new habits to find yourself back where you started. In many ways, succeeding in reaching a goal is a common cause of losing it just as fast.

If Not, What Did We Learn?

If you didn't achieve your goal, there is no need to get down on yourself. Instead, you should spend time trying to figure out why. As we discussed, maybe it wasn't clearly defined or given a clear deadline.

Another issue might be that your goal wasn't achievable. It was simply too large a problem for you to overcome. This comes back to our second PowerList™. You need to set reasonable goals. However, sometimes you don't know what is reasonable until you try to achieve it. For all you know, you might have set your goal so low that achieving it didn't even give you a rush.

What Can We Change for the Next Round?

Failure is a natural part of learning. So don't be too hard on yourself. Rather, focus on making the changes you need in order to succeed next time. In fact, the same factors influence failure when focusing on different types of goals. The ability to see the reason for failure will directly affect your ability to achieve more than this particular goal.

For example, maybe you didn't follow your PowerList™ for your daily checklist. You forgot to do it for a week or so. That might indicate that you need to put a reminder on the calendar to start your daily checklist.

Another trick for this is choosing your password for your computer accounts. Set a password like "DidIDoMyDailyChecklist5." It's a good password and will remind you of the things that matter when it comes to reaching your goal.

Creating/Using PowerList™ #8: Evaluation List

The PowerList™ #8 is critical since it will determine what happens next. This list is where you write down your lessons learned. In the template, it should include what went right, what went wrong, and what changes you will make next time.

Even if everything went great, there are always areas that can be finely tuned. You should see any issues you faced on the barriers list. After all, the point of the barriers list was to ensure you have an overview of what is stopping you from following the system and reaching your goal.

Patterns Are Clues

Sometimes, when things go well or poorly for us, we assume that it was because of something we did when in reality it may have nothing to do with that. As humans, we are looking for patterns.

In fact, it is difficult to not look for patterns in what we do and draw connections between our actions in a given area and the outcome of those actions. Many times we might see direct cause and effect relationships. For example, we were trying to lose weight. So, we ate less and exercised more. We found that after a few months we lost the weight. This connection isn't hard to find.

On the other hand, sometimes we get lucky. When someone is successful and tells us the secret of their success, that approach may not work for anyone else. This may be because timing is everything and they got lucky. They succeeded in a different time and they are a different person. Perhaps the trick that worked for them isn't going to be the trick that works for us.

A more useful approach is to find others who have failed at particular tasks and see if you can find reflections from them on why they think they failed and see if that applies to you.

Example

PowerList™ #8: Evaluation List			
#	Goal	What went right?	What went wrong	Changes to be made next time?
1	Lose 15 lb.	I hit the gym every day		No change required
2			I ate junk food	I need better accountability
3		I decreased TV and computer time		I could cut out even more time
4			I got burned out on the gym	Try going hiking or walks
5				

13 - Ready for Your Next Goal?

After seeing that I had achieved my goal regarding weight loss BMI (Body Mass Index) of 20, there was a question, "What next?" I didn't want to go any lower than BMI 20, but was there a next step to be taken? Or maybe I should be happy with the goal reached and stop looking for a new goal?

Is It Time for a New Goal?

So, you created your list of things that went right and wrong. In addition, you identified the reasons for the success or failure and you made comments on what you will do different next time. At this point, you are ready to move on to the final step.

Part of this process will depend upon whether or not you reached your goal. Now comes the tricky part. Even if you didn't achieve your goal, you may not wish to keep moving in that direction. Sometimes trying to achieve a goal can give you a confirmation about whether or not you ought to strive for the goal in the first place.

Some goals simply come at too high a price to family, friends, or ourselves. That must be taken into consideration. As we discussed on the goal setting PowerList™ chapter, it is hard to know what the costs of working toward a goal will be until you try it yourself. However, it may be helpful to hear from other people about their experiences.

For example, maybe your goal is to become a professional artist. You did your research and knew that it wasn't going to be easy, but you gave it a go. You created a task list including the buying of materials and signed up for the necessary courses. On your daily list, you listed doing homework for those courses and producing content.

In addition, you set up a website and attended networking groups with other artists in the area. After a year, you realize that you aren't selling anything. It is very disappointing, but you have actually tried it and have done all of the tricks to making this goal a reality.

In this example, the right choice may, in fact, be to give up the goal. It depends upon how much you want it. If you did your evaluation correctly, you should have an idea of what your chances are if you continue another round with this goal. Your evaluation list will give you enough information to see if trying again will produce a different result.

There is never any need to feel shame because you failed to reach your goal. The world is full of people who never tried. Failure is extremely important in figuring out what works for you and what doesn't. It is like a sculptor chipping away stone that isn't needed.

Therefore, failure helps confirm what goals simply aren't worth your time or aren't achievable. At the same time, by clearing them from your list of goals, you are one step closer to achieving goals that are worth the effort.

Finally, let's assume you either reached your goal or decided that you don't wish to continue working on your goal. This means it is time for a new goal. So, how do we go about moving in that direction? Well, the answer is simple. You go back to the beginning of this book and start over.

However, you aren't starting from scratch. Your previous lists are already in place and you have built a system that you have already used. Now it is a matter of updating the lists based upon what you learned. You, as a person, have also changed since you are becoming a person of habit and the steps get easier each time they are followed.

Quick Review

In summary, I have now gone through the steps to developing your PowerLists™ and given you the information and tools you need to succeed. In review, here are the steps:

- Self-assessment

- Goal Setting

- Goal Road Map

- Daily Checklists

- Task Management System

- The Calendar

- Motivation

- Barriers

- Evaluation

Closing Thoughts

It isn't easy to reach your goals. Anyone who tells you it is, isn't telling you the truth. Don't be hard on yourself when you fail. Failure is extremely important in reaching and achieving goals in life.

However, you should not let those failures lead you to believe that you can't achieve your goals. Rather, failure gives you an opportunity to go back through your PowerLists™ and make changes necessary to ensure success next time.

I hope you enjoyed this book and I hope it has given you a great starting point toward achieving your goals.

Thank You

As we reach the end of this book, I want to say thanks for reading this book.

I want to get this information out to as many people as possible. If you found this book helpful, I would greatly appreciate you leaving me a review. This helps others find the book as well.

This book was self-published with the amazing help of Self-Publishing Made Easy Now! [22] . You can grab a free copy of the checklist that started my journey here: FREE Self-Publishing Checklist [23] .

[22]https://selfpublishingmadeeasynow.com/xpjv
[23]https://selfpublishingmadeeasynow.com/free_checklist

Disclaimer

This document is geared towards providing exact and reliable information in regards to the topic and issue covered. The publication is sold on the idea that the publisher is not required to render an accounting, officially permitted, or otherwise, qualified services. If advice is necessary, legal, financial, medical or professional, a practiced individual in the profession should be ordered.

This information is not presented by a financial or medical practitioner and is for entertainment, educational and informational purposes only. The content is not intended as a substitute for professional medical advice, diagnosis, or treatment. Always seek the advice of your physician or other qualified health care provider with any questions you may have regarding a medical condition. Never disregard professional medical advice or delay in seeking it because of something you have read.

The information provided herein is stated to be truthful and consistent, in that any liability, in terms of inattention or otherwise, by any usage or abuse of any policies, processes,

DISCLAIMER

or directions contained within is the solitary and utter responsibility of the recipient reader. Under no circumstances will any legal responsibility or blame be held against the publisher for any reparation, damages, or monetary loss due to the information herein, either directly or indirectly.

www.ingramcontent.com/pod-product-compliance
Lightning Source LLC
Chambersburg PA
CBHW060338130626
46553CB00003B/1039